40 DAYS OF GOING DEEPER WITH GOD

MARY SWAIN

ISBN (paperback): 978-1-7395233-2-9
ISBN (eBook): 978-1-7395233-3-6

In accordance with the author's preference, pronouns referring to God, Jesus or the Holy Spirit have been capitalised.

Cover design and typesetting by Jbookdesigns

Mary Swain
Website: www.maryswain.co.uk
Contact: mary@maryswain.co.uk

Endorsements

'I was really honoured to be asked to endorse Mary's new book. I feel her hunger to pursue God for more is beautifully demonstrated throughout the pages of this latest offering.

Mary's examples from scripture are so relatable to our own lives as we journey through challenges, navigating our decisions, direction and the bumps in the road.

This book is full of optimism, encouraging us to lean into the Lord, staying resolute and focussed on Him whilst remaining honest and vulnerable in the process. I love the way she encourages us to use our sanctified imaginations to engage with Jesus in conversation, welcoming His Presence right there with us as a daily intentional practice.

Listening to Him, giving His Presence our priority, which in itself is our gift to Him, rather than a physical act that demonstrates our busyness working for Him.

I do encourage readers to spend time dwelling on the principles Mary highlights for us. They are not only relevant, but also profoundly impactful when grasped and activated.

There are gems here that are transformational, and I do not hesitate in recommending this book to all of us, whatever point we are at on our own spiritual walk.'

Veronica Mee – National Director,
Healing Rooms England & Wales

'These inspiring and insightful reflections on going deeper with God are not to be skim read! Mary's uniquely creative writings give opportunity for the reader to take time to pause and reflect to discover a greater awareness of God's personhood and presence in everyday life.'

Linda Harding – Advisor on international mission, mentor, coach, and leader

'We've enjoyed reading Mary's devotions, and what we've seen in these readings is the ability to bring practical theology into practical lifestyle.

It's a great joy to be able to learn from Mary's thoughts on how she's outworking it, but also inspiring us to put it into our everyday practice.

These devotions will enrich and support and nourish one's spiritual journey, as well as demonstrating how that person can live faith out in their everyday circumstances.'

Ben Jones – CEO of Missional Generation

This book is devoted to my wonderful family.
Each day I grow more and more grateful for you all! I am so blessed that I get to go on this journey of life with you.

Acknowledgements

Keith, thank you for your meticulous proofreading! Dayspring Church, thank you for always supporting me and reading my various writings. I'm so grateful to be part of such a wonderful church family.

Contents

Introduction

When a baby is born, there is an incredible journey that lies ahead of them of growing up and growing into the person they are made to be. Babies don't stay as babies: with nurture and care, they grow in stature and maturity each day.

When we first decide to follow Jesus, we are born again. However, so many Christians just stay there! There is a whole journey of growing, learning and maturing in Christ that awaits us.

Our lives here on earth are not a waiting game until eventually we die and go to heaven. The adventure starts now! As a Christian, you are not just living in your own story, but you play a part in the eternal story of God. This story is happening right now and you are part of it. What a privilege to be grafted into the narrative of the Almighty God!

I have found that the deeper I go in my relationship with God, the more this relationship becomes both an immovable foundation in my life and an ever increasing joy each day. Therefore, I want to share some of my thoughts and reflections to encourage you to go deeper with God too!

There is no right or wrong way to read this book. You could read one devotion each day for 40 days, or you could dip in and out at different times.

There is a response section at the end of each devotion which encourages you to engage with Father God, Jesus and the Holy Spirit about what you have read. There are no rules when it comes to how you respond! Have a read of my guidance and questions, but most importantly, have a chat with God and listen to Him!

Listening to God's voice might seem daunting or complicated, but like learning a language, it often just takes practice to familiarise yourself with the sounds and patterns. God is your good Father and He wants to speak to you and guide you, so He will not make it overly difficult! All He wants is your listening ear.

As you listen to God, you might want to write and journal God's voice, to draw, to look and see what He is showing you, to close your eyes and use your imagination, to sit still and pay attention to the impressions He is giving you, or to get up and move around. You have a personal relationship with God, so the way He talks to you will be personal as well.

I hope and pray you enjoy the journey of going deeper with God and that each day, you may become more and more captivated by how wonderful He is!

Fresh Hope

'He gives strength to the weary and increases the power of the weak. Even youths grow tired and weary, and young men stumble and fall; but those who hope in the Lord will renew their strength. They will soar on wings like eagles; they will run and not grow weary, they will walk and not be faint.'

Isaiah 40:29-31

I used to recite these verses when I was at dance college and the teacher would say, *"One more time!"* Lord, give me the strength to get through this!

When reading these verses again, it struck me that the key here is hope.

'Those who hope in the Lord will renew their strength.' (Isaiah 40:31)

Hope is powerful. The hope we have as Christians is not just wishful thinking. Positivity and optimism might work for a time, but true hope can remain in any circumstance.

There's a temptation to think that we shouldn't be too hopeful because we will just get let down or disappointed. Maybe past circumstances have made you cautious to dream again for fear of disappointment. Maybe it seems a bit pointless to try and hope again. That could be the case if we put our hope in organisations or leaders or movements because none of us are perfect.

But when we hope in Jesus, our hope is sure. The glimpse we have of His kingdom is only a tiny taste of what is to come. He will surpass all our hopes and dreams for all of eternity.

Psalm 25:3 says: *'No one who hopes in you will ever be put to shame.'*

It is not foolish or thoughtless to have hope. Jesus *is* victorious and there is nothing that can stop His kingdom from coming. Hope that is rooted in Him, no matter how small, cannot be squashed!

No matter how much bad news I hear or how many things go wrong, I am determined that I will always hope in the Lord. He is the only constant. He is our rock.

So, *'May the God of hope fill you with all joy and peace as you trust in him, so that you may overflow with hope by the power of the Holy Spirit.' (Romans 15:13)*

RESPONSE

Spend some time with Jesus now and allow yourself to be refreshed. Allow His presence to wash over you. As you rest in Him and behold His power and beauty, allow hope to rise up — a hope that is rooted in who He is.

Think about your hopes and dreams. Bring them before God now. They are important to Him! What does He want to say about them? What encouragement does He have for you today?

Maybe due to circumstances, you are cautious to dream or hope again. Ask Jesus if there is some disappointment in your life. You may want to do a symbolic act of placing this in His hands. Let Him give you fresh hope in place of this disappointment. This may be something that takes time. Is there someone you need to talk to about this to help you journey through disappointment?

Tuna Sandwiches

'For he satisfies the thirsty and fills the hungry with good things.'

Psalm 107:9

I was helping out with a children's holiday club last summer. Every day at lunchtime, we served up lots of sandwiches and there was one boy in particular who LOVED tuna sandwiches! Whilst everyone was still eating, he had already finished and asked if he could have more. We always had some extra made up in the kitchen, so when he asked, we'd bring out another plate. Most days he had at least three rounds of tuna sandwiches!

Some children had one sandwich and were satisfied so we didn't give them any more, but because we still had extra sandwiches, we loved it when someone did ask for more. This boy had the boldness to keep asking, so it was our joy to keep giving!

This story makes me smile because it reminds me of the Father's joy in giving us good things when we ask. I think He likes us to ask Him for things because He knows He has more than enough to satisfy our hunger!

Jesus asked blind Bartimaeus: *'What do you want me to do for you?' (Mark 10:51)*

I can imagine Jesus' pleasure in posing this question because He knew that if Bartimaeus asked to see, Jesus would absolutely be able to satisfy his request!

Jesus also asks that same question to James and John in Mark 10:36: *'What do you want me to do for you?'*

James and John asked to sit at Jesus' right and left in His glory. There were self-seeking motives behind their request that they needed to examine, and Jesus responded by saying this was not for Him to grant. However, afterwards, I think Jesus might have smiled to Himself at their boldness to actually ask this!

Is it better to have that kind of freedom and boldness in coming before God with our requests, or to never ask anything at all and therefore not receive?

I think we should carefully examine our motives behind what we are asking, but we also shouldn't shy away from asking for things. Our Father delights in satisfying our requests. We will never know if we don't ask!

RESPONSE

Take a moment to examine your view of God. Do you see Him as a generous Father who is excited to give you good gifts? If not, ask God where you might be believing a lie about Him. Ask Him to show you the truth about His character instead.

Do you ask God when you need help? Is He your first point of call? It's good to talk with others and lean on their support, but don't forget that the Holy Spirit is also called the Helper. What do you need help with today?

Imagine Jesus standing in front of you. Hear Him say to you, '*What do you want me to do for you?*' What's your response?

Sitting At His Feet

'She had a sister called Mary, who sat at the Lord's feet listening to what he said.'

Luke 10:39

Mary sat at Jesus' feet. She soaked up His words and His teaching. She spent time just listening to Him and being with Him. Her just sitting there was a gift to Jesus. She recognised who Jesus truly was, and it was an act of adoration towards Him.

I have often thought about this story in relation to what the sisters gained or missed out on. Martha missed out on the words of Jesus and time with Him because she was too busy, but Mary learnt more and gained more from soaking up Jesus' words.

Martha missed out on experiencing the peace of Jesus. He said to Martha: *'You are worried and upset about many things.' (Luke 10:41)*

I don't know about you, but I can identify with that feeling of being worried and upset about many things! Mary didn't seem to be worried and upset because her focus was on Jesus, and in His presence there is peace. Even when there are things to do, we can always find peace in the presence of Jesus.

But rather than focussing on what we can gain from Jesus, what about what Jesus wants? Does He want food? Or does He want our hearts?

Martha's gift of well prepared food I'm sure was gratefully received. Jesus enjoyed a feast! But Mary's gift was her heart that was postured towards Him. This was a beautiful thing to Jesus and it meant more to Him than anything anyone could do for Him.

At a time when there was much debate about who Jesus was, it seemed that Mary recognised Him as the King, as God and as her Lord. She showed this through her actions. She understood the gravity of the fact that King Jesus was in her midst and she honoured Him with her time and her heart posture.

Every time we choose to just be with Jesus, it is a beautiful thing. It's a gift. How wonderful when God's children recognise Jesus as Lord like Mary did! How wonderful when we honour Jesus just for who He is.

So, your food is gratefully received, but your heart is what He wants.

RESPONSE

Take some time today to recognise Jesus in your midst. Recognise Him as Lord. Recognise Him as the God of the universe, here with you. What other names of Jesus do you want to choose to recognise Him as today?

Take some time to examine your heart. Do you spend your time doing things for Jesus or just being with Him? Does worry and stress easily take over? If so, how can you prioritise His presence to shift your focus to what is really important? Remember, He is not condemnatory! He loves you and wants to spend more time with you!

'You are my daily bread
I never have to beg
You keep me hungry
You keep me fed' [1]

Sometimes, we might be spiritually busy. There are so many things to pray about, so many different Bible passages to read, and so many different things to learn from people around us.

It is good practice to come to God and simply ask, "Lord, what do you have for me today? What is my daily bread?"

This has helped me to lean into what He has for me in that moment. It doesn't mean there is no room for the things that I want to discuss and bring before God, but it helps me to be continually led by Him and not by my agenda.

I like to picture that Jesus' physical and spiritual provision for us each day is almost like a big advent calendar where there is a door for every day of our life! He has blessing and provision stored up for us each and every day. There is not one day that is empty. We don't always know what is to come, but we do know that He has a plan and a purpose for each day.

He has good things for you today. He will have good things for you tomorrow too!

---

[1] Elyssa Figueroa (2021) 'Daily Bread' from the album *'Wearing A Blindfold And Running'*.

Daily Bread

'Man shall not live on bread alone, but on every word that comes from the mouth of God.'

Deuteronomy 8:3 / Matthew 4:4

There is a wonderful theme of daily bread that is found all throughout the Bible. We see the Isrealites in the wilderness receiving daily provision from God: just enough for each day. Jesus teaches us to pray for our daily bread with the expectation that God does have exactly what we need for that day.

Jesus also says: *'I am the bread of life. Whoever comes to me will never go hungry, and whoever believes in me will never be thirsty.' (John 6:35)*

This image of bread symbolises both our physical needs and our spiritual needs.

There is a beautiful, simple song by Elyssa Figueroa called 'Daily Bread'. These are the lyrics:

RESPONSE

Come before Jesus today. Ask Him, "What is it that you have for me today, Jesus? What is my daily bread?" Follow His lead. Maybe there is a picture He wants to show you, something He wants to tell you or something He wants you to read. Or maybe He just wants you to sit with Him and be with Him today.

Listen to the song 'Daily Bread' by Elyssa Figueroa, or just take some time to read the lyrics. Soak in the words of this song. Let the truth of God go deep in your spirit. Rest in God being your perfect Provider in every way.

Leading Yourself

'Praise the Lord, my soul; all my inmost being, praise his holy name.'

Psalm 103:1

Have you ever been in a place where you are surrounded by people who are hungry for God and it's just easy to worship Him? The music and atmosphere is just right, there are no distractions, and you are led into the presence of God.

I believe it's really important to seek out these places where others are hungry for God. Corporate worship and seeking God's face together is all part of God's design and plan for us.

I also believe that one of the marks of being a mature Christian is being able to lead yourself into encounter. What happens when there's no one there to strike up the band? What happens when it's just you and God?

David knew how to stir himself to worship God. Countess times throughout the psalms, he talks to his own being and leads himself to a place of praise and thankfulness. He first learns to lead himself, and then he can lead others.

It's not just in worship that this is important, but it's also about learning to lead yourself to get your strength from God. When David was in crisis — Ziklag was destroyed and everyone was against him — David led himself into communion with God.

> *'But David found strength in the Lord his God.'*
> *(1 Samuel 30:6)*

We could try and get strength and encouragement from other places, but true strength comes directly from God. I believe it takes practice and perseverance to keep leading ourselves into this secret place with God where we are refreshed and refilled by Him.

It's one of those things that no one else can do for us, but we all must learn individually how to manage our daily relationship with God. We need to learn to draw on God's strength in the difficult times, but also to keep leading ourselves to lean on God even when everything is going well.

I believe that the more we practise leading ourselves in the secret place, the hungrier we will become for God's presence.

RESPONSE

How do you feel about leading yourself in your relationship with God? Do you rely on others or can you lead yourself? Does it depend on how you are feeling in the moment?

What brings you into a place of worship? It's okay to think of particular ways to stir yourself and lead yourself into this place. It could be saying the names of God. It could be just becoming aware of His closeness to you. It could be thinking about things you are thankful for or rejoicing in testimonies of God's faithfulness to you and others. It could be adopting a posture of worship. Use these things to lead yourself into a place of praise.

When you need strength, do you go to God, or do you seek it in other places? Have a conversation with God about it. What does it look like for you to draw on God's strength wherever you are right now? How can you discipline and lead yourself to do this?

Refiner's Fire

'I will refine them like silver and test them like gold. They will call on my name and I will answer them; I will say, 'They are my people,' and they will say, 'The Lord is our God.''

Zechariah 13:9

When silver or gold is refined, it needs to be heated up to around 1000 degrees Celsius in order for the impurities to be removed. That's pretty hot!

In the Bible, there are many instances comparing God's work in us to being like a refiner's fire: an extremely hot furnace that burns off anything that is impure.

God made us perfectly. At our core we are like the pure silver or gold. Through life, we might take on impurities, like lies that we end up believing or sinful habits. God wants to remove these things so we can have fullness of life with Him.

The way to remove impurities is fire. It could feel like we are being burned up because maybe these impurities have become part of our identity or our way of thinking, but the pure silver or gold will not be consumed by the fire. It will emerge as pure, the way God intended us to be.

It may feel uncomfortable and painful, but ultimately as God's children, we are attracted to this fire because we know it is good.

In the verse at the top, God refines the remnant. He refines the ones who remain close to Him. The refining results in a new intimacy with God and a security of identity rooted in the knowledge of Him. How wonderful to be purified and drawn closer by the Creator Himself!

It's important to recognise God's refining fire in our lives because when we recognise His fire, we can then rest, knowing that this is a good place to be. It is a place that will result in more purity and intimacy. We can submit to the work of God in us and work with Him, knowing that His fire is love.

Submitting to His good work in us, we can then say in confidence: *'But he knows the way that I take; when he has tested me, I will come forth as gold.' (Job 23:10)*

RESPONSE

Have you been aware of God's refining fire in your life? Can you think back to a time when in the moment, it seemed uncomfortable, but you have emerged with greater purity of heart, intimacy and strength?

Ask God to show you how He is refining you at the moment. See this refining through His lens of love. How can you submit to Him and work with Him in this refining? Rejoice that He is drawing you closer to Him.

Ask God if there is any way in which you have resisted His refining. Is there anything He wants you to do to work with Him?

Passing By

'Jesus of Nazareth is passing by.'
Luke 18:37

I don't have a car, so I do quite a lot of walking. Often, I have a destination that I am heading to and will walk to get there. However, sometimes I like going on a walk just for the sake of walking! The fun is in the journey, not in a particular destination.

Jesus did a lot of walking. When we read the Bible, we can go from passage to passage quickly, but the reality for Jesus wasn't so quick! For example, Jesus meets Zacchaeus while He was passing through Jericho at the beginning of Luke 19, but by the end of the chapter He is in Jerusalem. That's 18 miles and quite a climb up the Mount of Olives! He didn't just click His fingers and arrive. He took every step along the way.

Jesus' ministry was all a journey. Many times in the Bible, Jesus is described as *'passing by'. (John 1:36) (Mark 6:48) (Luke 19:1) (Luke 24:28)*

Even if He was heading towards a particular destination, each step and each person along the way was important. The people in the background became main characters in His story as He allowed Himself to be interrupted. (Read Matthew 8 and 9 for many examples of people encountering Jesus on His journey!)

Jesus often allowed Himself to be taken seemingly off course, even though it wasn't really off course at all. On His ministry journey, His goal was to do and say and join in with what His Father was doing and He did this at every step, not just at the destination points.

We can sometimes be very destination focussed. It's a good thing to have a plan and to head in that direction, but we also mustn't neglect the journey. There will be things that God wants to show us and teach us along the way.

So let's place significance on the journey we are on as well as on the marker points. With God, joy can be found in every step!

RESPONSE

This may be a good time to have a look at some of the goals that you have in mind. Take some time to consider your priorities and have a chat about them with Jesus.

Is your primary goal to get to a particular place? Or is it to be like Jesus along the way? Is it to achieve a certain thing, or is it to do everything with Him in mind and for His glory? We all have different goals so we shouldn't compare these with other people, but it is good to evaluate our priorities and motives. Do you place value on the journey as well as on the significant marker moments?

What is your vision statement for your life? Why are you here? What is your purpose? Take some time with Jesus to write something down. What does it look like to live that vision statement at every step along the journey of your life?

To Know And Be Known

'Now this is eternal life: that they know you, the only true God, and Jesus Christ, whom you have sent.'

John 17:3

God is our destination. When we believe in Jesus, it's not just about someday going to heaven, but our destination is God Himself. That means that we are not just wandering around and waiting until we die to enter into eternal life, but eternal life starts now because God is with us.

Relationship with God is what it is all about! We may do exciting things with Him along the way, but these things are not the ultimate goal.

When you spend time with family or friends, you don't spend time with them just to get something out of it. In healthy relationships, you spend time with other people because you enjoy their company and you love them.

It is sobering to think of how much of our relationship with God can be transactional. Even if we don't realise it, it is so easy to fall into using worship or time spent in prayer as a means to get something from Him.

The Holy Spirit is our Helper and there are many things that He does, but He is not just a functional being. He is a person of God.

When we seek relationship with the Spirit above all else, it no longer looks like the Holy Spirit just working alongside us when we ask Him to, but it looks like Him working in and through us wherever we go.

How wonderful to think that the God of the universe wants to be with us and work through us! He is unfathomable yet knowable. He is everywhere, and yet He is sitting here with you. He is sovereign over all, yet He is still patient with us on our journeys.

Surely the most wonderful thing in the world is just to know and be known by God.

RESPONSE

Take some time now just to be aware of the Holy Spirit with you. Pay attention to Him and delight in knowing that He is here with you. Rest in this place.

As you rest in the presence of God, pay attention to your senses. God might want to let you feel His tangible presence. Can you see Him? Can you hear His heartbeat? Can you smell His beautiful fragrance? Whether you sense something or not, He is still there. Stay a little longer in His presence.

There's No Stopping Nehemiah

'They were all trying to frighten us, thinking, "Their hands will get too weak for the work, and it will not be completed." But I prayed, "Now strengthen my hands."'

Nehemiah 6:9

I love the story of Nehemiah! There are so many great things to learn from his journey when it comes to persevering in the face of opposition.

Poor Nehemiah was trying to lead a project of rebuilding the walls of Jerusalem whilst so many people kept telling him he wouldn't be able to do it! They tried everything to stop him: they ridiculed him, they threatened him with violence, and they even hired someone to appear as a prophet just to intimidate Nehemiah!

But none of this hindered the work or Nehemiah's attitude. I believe this is because Nehemiah was quick to recognise the voice of the enemy and see that it was not aligned with what God said. When he recognised the voice of the enemy, he went directly to God for strength. He chose to keep his eyes on his goal and he remembered the favour of God on him for this project. Strengthened by God, he had the tenacity to keep going.

Nehemiah also had creative solutions and strategies to stand against the opposition. He placed guards strategically around the walls and equipped the people with armour and weapons. He encouraged the people in the Lord and prayed continually.

The enemy might try to weaken us or talk us out of something, but Nehemiah shows us that we don't have to give in. It's even better for us living post-resurrection because we have the power of the Holy Spirit at work in us and through us.

Paul says: *'We are more than conquerors through him who loved us'*! *(Romans 8:37)*

Through God's power that is at work within us, we can overcome all the power of the enemy. If we feel weak, that's okay, because God is strong! All of our strength comes from Him and He won't let us down.

RESPONSE

Read Nehemiah chapter 4. Look at Nehemiah's responses to the opposition and how he encouraged the people. What can you learn and take away from his attitude and actions?

Is there a difficult situation that you are facing at the moment? Like Nehemiah, turn to God in prayer. Pray: *'Lord, strengthen my hands.'*

Are there any particular strategies that God wants to give you at this time to stand firm in His strength? Maybe it is setting aside time for worship. Maybe there is a particular Bible passage He wants you to hold on to in this season. Maybe He is encouraging you to gather with others to pray. Ask Him about it!

Reading The Word

'I rejoice in following your statutes as one rejoices in great riches. I meditate on your precepts and consider your ways. I delight in your decrees; I will not neglect your word.'

Psalm 119:14-16

It's a wonderful gift that the Bible is so readily available to us! In Medieval England, if you couldn't speak Latin and if you weren't a leader in the church, you couldn't really get access to a Bible. But now, we can all have copies and read them whenever we like!

The Bible is probably the only book that we will continually read throughout our lives. I like reading a good book maybe a second time, but any more than that and it spoils the enjoyment (for me, anyway!)

The good thing about the Bible is that it is living and active. You might know from experience that the fruit and revelation you get from the Bible increases the deeper you dive into it!

However, I know that sometimes I can easily lose the excitement when reading the Bible. Especially with stories I've read a lot of times, I can easily skim over them without allowing the truth to unfold and develop my understanding.

The Word is a constant that never changes and never gets old. But in those times when we know we need to be a bit more intentional about studying the Word, we can be creative in our approach!

Sometimes to change up my patterns, I like to read a whole book at once to see the bigger picture, or do a deep dive into just one verse and stay with it for a while. You could read in a different translation for a change, listen to the Bible being read, or speak it out instead of reading in your head. You could paint verses and memorise them as you do, find songs where the lyrics are scripture, or write your own songs!

Creative approaches and changing our patterns of reading the Bible can help us to adopt the Word into our whole being and keep the wonder and excitement of the Word of God.

RESPONSE

What is your appetite like for reading the Word at the moment? If you are feeling like you have lost your hunger, a good first step is to acknowledge this and to talk to Jesus about this. Ask Him what He wants to say about His Word. Ask Him to renew your appetite for delving into the Bible.

Out of some of the different ideas listed in this devotion for reading the Bible, is there one of these that you could try out in order to switch up your routine and approach the Bible in a new way? Do something different to engage with the Word of God today. See how it goes!

Which Way?

> 'Trust in the Lord with all your heart and lean not on your own understanding; in all your ways submit to him, and he will make your paths straight.'
>
> Proverbs 3:5-6

Sometimes when you have a decision to make, there may be a moral right way and a moral wrong way. Sometimes, both options in front of you are good, but one is just better. But have you ever been faced with a decision to make where it seems like both choices could be right and in alignment with God's plans and you just feel a bit stuck?

When I was 18, I was trying to decide which dance college to go to. I had two good options in front of me and the decision was in my hands. I kept going backwards and forwards between the two but just felt overwhelmed by the decision.

Someone at my church prayed that God would give me a big, yellow, flashing sign! She said she felt God was saying, "You will know, you will know, you will know."

"Great!" I thought. But a couple of weeks went by and I still didn't know, didn't know, didn't know, nor had I seen any big, yellow, flashing signs.

Then one day, I was listening to a podcast and the person speaking said, "You will know, you will know, you will know … if it is wrong."

Hmm. That was a big, yellow, flashing sign, but not the one I wanted! This meant I had to choose without fully knowing if it was the "right" decision. But it seemed that God was giving me permission to just choose, so I did.

It turned out that when I stepped into that college and community, it became more and more apparent that it was a good place for me to be. It wasn't necessarily about it being the right place and the other place being completely wrong, but it was a good decision, and I knew it wasn't wrong.

I have found that with life decisions, often there isn't one particular right way to go, but there will be a right way to *go about* things. Whichever decision you make, go about it prayerfully. Go about it in relationship with other people. Have good, honouring conversations. It doesn't necessarily matter *what* you choose, but it does matter who you *are*. With good character and a strong relationship with God, you can't go too far wrong!

RESPONSE

Do you have a decision that you are facing at the moment? First of all, is there a way which is morally wrong which you should avoid? If not, is there a way that you just know is better than the other way? If you are faced with two options that could be equally good, ask Jesus how He wants you to go about making this decision.

Talk with Him about the different options. What does He have to say about them? Talk with other people about the options. Ultimately, don't be afraid to actually make a choice. What do you want to do?

God With Us

'But very truly I tell you, it is for your good that I am going away. Unless I go away, the Advocate will not come to you; but if I go, I will send him to you.'

John 16:7

When Jesus died, His followers' hopes and dreams were completely and utterly shattered. Everything they had envisioned, planned and hoped for came crashing down to nothing.

But we know how the story goes: they went from the deepest despair to complete elation when they saw that Jesus had risen from the dead!

Phew, it's all going to be okay now! Better than just okay!

I can imagine they thought: "Now Jesus is alive again, even more people will believe! We can go to all the people who accused Him and prove them wrong! Now they will have to believe He's the Son of God!"

But Jesus said: *'Do not hold on to me, for I have not yet ascended to the Father.' (John 20:17)*

What? He's going again? Talk about a rollercoaster of emotions.

Jesus had bigger plans. In the verse at the top, He said it is for our good that He is going away because it meant the Holy Spirit could come.

Walking with Jesus on the earth like the disciples did must have been incredible. But the reality is, we are actually much better off now because Jesus ascended. Jesus the man could only be in one place at any one time. Now, we have the Holy Spirit with us who is fully God and fully present everywhere. We each have the Advocate, Helper, Counsellor and Comforter with us.

The Holy Spirit is not just someone who helps us connect to Jesus. He is God Himself. He is moving right here on the earth in great strength and power and He is readily available to all of us. It's really up to us how much we engage with Him.

So remember, we are living in the days of "God with us"! What a privilege!

RESPONSE

Do you ever see the Holy Spirit as lesser to Jesus or to Father God, even unintentionally? Take some time now to ask the Holy Spirit to reveal Himself to you in a new way. Listen to Him. What does He want to show you about Himself? What does He want you to know about His availability?

Do you want to learn more about the Holy Spirit? Do you have a hunger to grow closer to Him? If so, is there something you could do to help you on this journey? Maybe there is someone you could talk to, a book you could read, a course you could take, or something you could build into your daily routine to help you listen to Him.

How Well Did You Love?

'By this everyone will know that you are my disciples, if you love one another.'

John 13:35

Recently, someone shared with me a situation that they were in and asked me to pray with them, which I did. Then, as I was walking home after praying with this person, I was pridefully thinking about how successfully I had implemented my prayer training. Thankfully, God interrupted my thoughts!

"But how well did you actually love them?"

Hmm. I realised that although I had ticked all the boxes in the "textbook", I was so quick to diagnose and fix that I forgot to love.

God's native language is love. If we want to reveal Him to others, make a difference, steward revelation or be part of ushering in the kingdom of God, we must learn to be people of love. If we want to share His heart authentically, we must learn to love like Him. The only way we can deliver a word of encouragement, wisdom or prophecy in its pure form is if we do it in love.

I had another experience not long ago where I prayed for someone, but this time, I intentionally took time to connect to God's heart and see them through the lens of His love. I wasn't very eloquent or impressively insightful, but the person ended up being really touched. It wasn't because of what I said, but because of God's love.

A wise person once told me that the goal in prayer and prophecy isn't to be the most accurate, but it's to love people well: to love people like Jesus. Practising to be more accurate is good, but it shouldn't come before love.

Jesus talks a lot about love. Love should be our team badge: a way in which people can recognise believers! Keep putting on your lenses of love to see people as God sees them!

RESPONSE

Think about a situation you were in recently where you had a conversation with a friend or where you prayed for someone. Ask yourself the question, "How well did I love?" This isn't to be overly critical, but just to reflect on how we are ambassadors of Jesus, showing His love.

Think about a situation you have coming up that involves some conversation with another person. Maybe it's coffee with a friend or a work meeting. Spend some time asking God to help you show love to this person. Be intentional when it comes to listening to them and encouraging them. Ask God to help you see them through His eyes.

Next time you're praying with someone, first take a moment to connect to the Father's heart. Ask God, "How do You see this person? How can I share Your heart with them?"

Teachable

'Listen to advice and accept instruction, that you may gain wisdom in the future.'

Proverbs 19:20 (ESV)

In the kingdom of God, being teachable is essential. It looks like being open, inviting, eager to learn and humble in heart.

There rightly is an emphasis on being teachable when you are younger. Wisdom is a gift from God, but it also grows with life experience, so it is wise to learn from those who have more life experience than you! It is important to be continually and intentionally open to the leading and counsel of those who are older.

We must also be open to the counsel of the Holy Spirit every day of our lives. We never graduate from learning and being guided by God! Being teachable in our walk with God is not about arriving at a particular destination of knowledge and understanding, but about constantly journeying in relationship and in submission to God. God is always speaking, so there is always more to discover!

Jesus' disciples are great examples of people who were teachable. They were hungry for Jesus' words and they were (generally) quick to learn from their mistakes. Jesus didn't pick disciples who had it all together; He picked people who were teachable.

Even well into the book of Acts when the disciples were at the forefront of a move of God, they still remained teachable and open to the counsel of others and the Holy Spirit. They weighed and tested revelation and sat in discussions with other people to make decisions.

For example, in the midst of the wrestle and debate around whether or not the Gentiles should follow the Jewish laws in Acts 15, it says:

> *'So Paul and Barnabas were appointed, along with some other believers, to go up to Jerusalem to see the apostles and elders about this question.' (Acts 15:2)*

The leaders sought wise counsel from others in order to make the right decision. Pride could have led them to make the judgement call on their own, but their teachable spirit drove them to take time to listen and learn and discuss with others first.

Therefore, if we want to be used by God, being teachable is an essential quality. It is much more important than having gifts, knowledge or life experience.

RESPONSE

Ask God to examine your heart. What does it look like for you in this season to be open and inviting of the Spirit's wisdom and the wisdom of others? If there is a particular decision you need to make or something you are embarking on or going through at the moment, how does God want you to be open to the leading of His Spirit in this process? Is there another person that He is highlighting to you who you could discuss things with in order to get another wise perspective?

As we get older we do gain more life experience and we can learn from our past mistakes. But what does it look like to still be constantly dependent on the guiding of the Spirit? Even if you are going through something that you have been through before, what does it look like to still seek counsel from God about the right steps to take at this particular time?

Blameless Before Christ

'We are made right with God by placing our faith in Jesus Christ. And this is true for everyone who believes, no matter who we are.'

Romans 3:22 (NLT)

It's a great feeling when, for example, you've been outside in the rain or you've been exercising and then you come home and have a shower and put on fresh, clean clothes! You have the feeling of being renewed and refreshed.

Zechariah has an incredible vision of Joshua the high priest having his filthy clothes completely replaced with clean, white garments.

The angel of the Lord says: *'See, I have taken away your sin, and I will put fine garments on you.' (Zechariah 3:4)*

In the vision, Satan is standing by ready to accuse Joshua. However, in the presence of the Lord, Satan didn't even get to speak. He had no ground to accuse Joshua when the Lord was advocating for him. Even in the presence of the enemy, Joshua was in right standing before God and the enemy had no power.

Through Jesus, this is the story for all of us! By His death and resurrection, we can all stand blameless before God.

As Joshua stood there in his clean, white clothes, the Lord's charge to him was to walk in obedience. Joshua didn't need to do anything to pay for these clothes. He had no debt. He didn't need to make up for the Lord's gift to him. He just needed to move forwards from this place in complete obedience to God.

Jesus didn't make repentance and forgiveness complicated. When we repent and turn around to face Jesus, He has already dealt with and forgotten our sin. We sometimes over complicate things by thinking there must be something else we need to do, but grace is simple if we can accept it!

So, let's be confident in our right standing before God, and move forwards in obedience from this place!

> *'But now he has reconciled you by Christ's physical body through death to present you holy in his sight, without blemish and free from accusation — if you continue in your faith, established and firm, and do not move from the hope held out in the gospel.' (Colossians 1:22-23)*

RESPONSE

Have a read of Zechariah 3. There are so many wonderful things to take note of in this passage! Imagine yourself in the place of Joshua. See how the Lord fights for you. Imagine yourself being clothed with clean, white robes and standing in confidence before the Lord.

Is there something that you know you need to repent of today? Ask Jesus if there is anything He wants you to deal with. You don't need to go on a deep dive and search for something! Just be open to the Lord's conviction if it comes. When you feel ready, bring this before the Lord and say sorry. Accept His forgiveness. See yourself standing blameless before Him. How does He want you to move forwards in obedience from this place?

Learning The Nighttime Language

'In the last days, God says, I will pour out my Spirit on all people. Your sons and daughters will prophesy, your young men will see visions, your old men will dream dreams.'

Acts 2:17

How wonderful is it that God can speak to us through dreams? When we are at rest He chooses to bless us with His thoughts. He has designed sleep to refresh us but also to communicate with us. As it shows in the verse above, dreaming is a mark of the Spirit and it is to be expected in these last days!

In Jesus' time, there was a view that the day starts in the evening rather than the morning. I think this is a helpful way to see the day when we want to learn to hear from God through our dreams. We will then be more intentional with how we spend our evening and how we go to bed, being expectant to hear from God in the night. This communication with Him can then continue throughout the day!

There were many dreamers in the Bible. It's interesting that people like Joseph (Jacob's son), Daniel, or Joseph (earthly father of Jesus) all interpreted their own dreams, but many pharaohs and kings had to ask for interpretations. It's not wrong to ask other people to help you interpret your dreams, but I do believe that you as a child of God are the best interpreter of your own dreams.

Joseph says: *'Do not interpretations belong to God?' (Genesis 40:8)*

If interpretations belong to God, that's good news because you have the Spirit of God living inside you!

If you look at a dream dictionary, it will most likely say that a dog in a dream symbolises loyalty. It might do for some people, but when I was younger, I had a dream that a dog bit my legs off, and that certainly wasn't about loyalty, it was about fear!

It's important to ask, "What does this mean to me?" Build up your own dream dictionary with God.

It's a bit like learning a language. Over time, you recognise more patterns that help your understanding. The more time you spend asking God about your dreams, the more patterns you will recognise and ways in which He speaks to you individually!

RESPONSE

In my journey, when I started talking to God about hearing Him through my dreams, the first thing He told me to do was to have a notebook and pen by the side of my bed. It's important to honour the ways in which He speaks to us by writing things down. This also helps on the journey of hearing His voice because you can start to spot patterns.

If you don't normally remember your dreams, ask God to help you remember them, and take a step of faith by putting a notebook by your bed.

Can you think of a dream you had recently? If you haven't already, write it out and ask God what He wants to show you. What was your main emotion or feeling in the dream? What was your main action? Who else was there? What do these things mean to you? Enjoy the adventure of discovery with God.

Come To Jesus

"'Lord, if it's you," Peter replied, "tell me to come to you on the water."'

Matthew 14:28

In the story where Jesus walked on the water, did you know it was Peter's idea to step out onto the water with Him? Jesus didn't summon him out of the boat, He just went along with Peter's bold request!

In answer to Peter's question in the verse at the top, Jesus must have thought, "Well, I am the Lord, so I guess I should say 'come'!"

So that's what He said: *'Come'. (Matthew 14:29)*

Peter's only question here was about who Jesus was. The only thing that mattered in that moment was that Jesus was who He said He was. It wasn't him trying to show off in front of his friends, but from the nature of his question, it was simply all about the person of Jesus.

He didn't say, "Lord, if it's safe, tell me to come." His focus wasn't on the waves or on the actual walking on the water. It was just on coming to Jesus, no matter what was in front of him.

He didn't say, "Lord, if it's you, you can calm the storm." He wasn't focussed on what Jesus could do for him; he just wanted to be close to Him.

He didn't say, "Lord, if it's you, come and join us in the boat." Peter was willing to take a risk to join Jesus where He was.

I've often been taught to pray, "Come, Holy Spirit". This is good and we should keep doing this! But I want to shift our perspective a little.

What would it look like to say, "Lord, how can I come to You? I want to be where You are. I want to join in with what You're doing. I want to see things from Your perspective."

When Peter took his eyes off Jesus — the reason why he was doing what he was doing in the first place — fear took over and he sank. But Jesus immediately saved him. He didn't stand back and say, "Well it was your idea to do this anyway!" He just brought Peter even closer to Him. Of course He did!

RESPONSE

The next time you are in worship, try telling yourself, "Come to Him". Position yourself to meet Him where He is. Tell your heart and soul to come close to the Lord.

The next time you pray for someone, take a moment to ask Jesus what He is doing and see how you can join in with that. Is He wanting to release His prophetic word? Is He present to heal? Is He wanting to surround the person with peace?

The next time you are in a difficult situation, pause and ask Jesus to show you things from His perspective. Come to Him and sit a while. See how He sees things.

Right now, why not take a moment to come to Jesus? It doesn't have to look like anything in particular. Just posture yourself towards Him.

Old Paths Vs. Ancient Paths

'Stand at the crossroads and look; ask for the ancient paths, ask where the good way is, and walk in it, and you will find rest for your souls.'

Jeremiah 6:16

The people of God are called to follow the ancient paths. There are many places in the Bible that refer to following the ancient ways.

For example: *'They will rebuild the ancient ruins and restore the places long devastated; they will renew the ruined cities that have been devastated for generations.' (Isaiah 61:4)*

We are called to be people who *'rebuild the ancient ruins'* and *'raise up the age-old foundations' (Isaiah 58:12)* just like Nehemiah who restored the physical walls of Jerusalem, or David who restored extravagant devotion to God in Israel. They were pioneers in the new, but they followed the ancient paths at the same time. They sought the heart and the unchanging order of God which led them to the new paths.

I believe there is a distinction between following ancient paths and following old paths.

Old paths are carved by humans and although they are well trodden and they may be good routes, they do not lead to the new.

The ancient paths facilitate the new because they are in full alignment with the ways of God.

If we take an example from the Bible, the teachers of the law in Jesus' time were following old paths, while Jesus was following ancient paths. The religious leaders taught rules and regulations, but Jesus taught ancient principles of love, rhythms of rest and honour for one another that were in place from the very beginning of time. Jesus followed the ancient ways of His Father to call in the new era!

Following the ancients paths doesn't mean we can't embrace new technology or innovation. God wants us to grow and flourish and use our creativity to explore new things, but we should always keep the ancient principles of the kingdom of God as our guide as we move forwards into the new.

RESPONSE

Take a moment to examine your heart with God. Do you find comfort in old paths: traditions, rules and particular ways of doing things? Ask God to help you live from a place of relationship with Him rather than out of duty or because of tradition and religion.

Take some time to re-read Jeremiah 6:16 at the start of this devotion. Close your eyes and imagine yourself standing at a crossroads. You may want to bring a particular decision before God, or just picture yourself walking with God through life. Take a moment to stop and stand first of all. Then look at the paths: what are the different paths in front of you? Can you see where they lead? Ask God where the good way is. Listen to what He shows you. What does He want to say about these paths? Imagine yourself walking down one of the paths with God. What do you see?

The Long Journey Home

'Blessed are those whose strength is in you, whose hearts are set on pilgrimage. As they pass through the Valley of Baka, they make it a place of springs; the autumn rains also cover it with pools. They go from strength to strength, till each appears before God in Zion.'

Psalm 84:5-6

The Valley of Baka symbolises a dry and barren place. It also symbolises a valley of tears and of weeping. It's a place that we will all pass through in some way during our lifelong pilgrimage on this earth.

Psalm 126:5 says: *'Those who sow with tears will reap with songs of joy.'*

Tears are prayers. Tears carry seed. We weep for the lost and the sick. We weep because of what we do not see when it comes to the knowledge of God on the earth. Tears are okay and they are often necessary.

Yet in these verses, there is so much hope! There are important promises to hold on to!

God will cause the songs of joy to rise up. Tears are not the end of the story. You will reap a joyful harvest!

As we walk through the valley of tears, we do not walk alone and we do not walk in vain. With the Spirit of God in us, these dry places will become places of life.

In this pilgrimage of life, whether we are on the mountaintops or in the valleys, God journeys with us and helps us to walk through any terrain. Surely in time we will see the springs start to rise up in the dry places!

We don't need to do any sprinting, but we just need to keep following Him. With our eyes on Him, we will have the strength to keep moving. He will give us the strength to have faith in His promises that we will reap a joyful and fruitful harvest.

Eugene Peterson describes the Christian walk as: '*A long obedience in the same direction.*'[2]

So, let's set our hearts on a lifelong pilgrimage with one destination in mind. Our entire lives are a journey home. Even though our bodies may grow weaker, each day we go from strength to strength as we get closer and closer to the kingdom of God: our home forever.

---

[2] Eugene Peterson (1980) '*A Long Obedience in the Same Direction: Discipleship in an Instant Society*'.

RESPONSE

Take some time to meditate on the verses in this devotion. Take comfort in these words.

Picture yourself walking this pilgrimage of life. Ask God to show you where you are on your journey right now. What is the terrain like? In this place that you are passing through, what does God want you to know? What does He want to show you in this place?

Keep imagining your walk with God through life. Look ahead and see where the path is heading. Ask God to show you a glimpse of the path ahead.

Selah

'Be still, and know that I am God'
Psalm 46:10

The Hebrew word 'selah' appears 71 times in the book of Psalms and 3 times in Habakkuk. The interesting thing is, no one can be completely sure what it means. In my NIV Bible, the footnote says: *'a word of uncertain meaning'*.

It is likely that it is a musical term based on the type of psalms it appears in. It is also likely that it means to 'pause' because it always appears at the end of a thought or phrase. It could be a moment to praise and to turn ourselves to wonder. It could be a moment just to stop and behold the Lord.

I like to think of it as a breath. A little bit of expanding space.

I was out for a walk recently and as I was looking out across one of the fields, there was a single bird circling and swooping over the frost. Gradually, one by one, more birds came out of nowhere to join this first one in these swooping patterns.

They just kept coming! It was like they were all entering into a beautiful dance.

I enjoyed stopping to watch these birds for a while. It was like a little 'selah' in my walk: a simple moment to pause and to delight before I carried on along the path. It was a simple reminder of the wonderful Creator present with me on my walk.

These 'selah' moments appear all throughout our day if we can be attentive enough to recognise them. It could be in that first sip of coffee, or when you open your curtains to look outside in the morning. Maybe it's when you put your knife and fork down after the last bite of a meal, or the quiet moment in between songs when you are listening to music.

In these moments, just be aware of the presence of God with you. You don't need to do anything in particular. Just be aware of Him. Lean into His nearness. Delight in His smile over you.

RESPONSE

Take a moment to still yourself now. Wait for a moment, not to do anything in particular, but just to pause and be aware of God.

Look out for the 'selah' moments today and lean into them. If you are busy, can you be intentional about creating moments to just stop and pause? What changes when you become aware of God's presence with you?

It's A Bit Stormy Out There!

"In a little while I will once more shake the heavens and the earth, the sea and the dry land. I will shake all nations, and what is desired by all nations will come, and I will fill this house with glory,' says the Lord Almighty.'

Haggai 2:6-7

It's a bit stormy out there at the moment! There is a lot of shaking going on. Things that once seemed certain now seem unpredictable. There are many unsettling things that are happening around the world.

The writer of Hebrews quotes the prophet Haggai in saying: *'"Once more I will shake not only the earth but also the heavens." The words "once more" indicate the removing of what can be shaken — that is, created things — so that what cannot be shaken may remain.' (Hebrews 12:26-27)*

When there is shaking, the good news is that we can be confident in the thing that cannot be shaken: God's kingdom. There is nothing that can stop or hinder His kingdom from being established.

Rather than living in fear or in reaction to what is going on around us, the Bible says that we can live from a place of security in closeness to God. Because God cannot be shaken, we can get behind Him and also be secure.

David writes: *'I keep my eyes always on the Lord. With him at my right hand, I will not be shaken.' (Psalm 16:8)*

I also believe we need to give ourselves grace in difficult seasons. It's not always easy to be at peace in the middle of a storm!

With much fear and unsteadiness around us, we might knowingly or unknowingly go around carrying a kind of anxiety, uneasiness or heaviness in our bodies. But when we trust only in the Lord, we can experience tangible peace and our bodies and minds can rest.

The Bible is full of promises that the righteous will not be shaken. *(Psalm 55:22) (Psalm 112:6) (Psalm 125:1)* I don't think we should just take these promises as self-preservation and go into hiding, but we should hold on to them firmly as our hope so that we can live freely and boldly out of this confidence in God.

So in this season, let's get behind what God is doing and take refuge in Him.

RESPONSE

Ask God if you have knowingly or unknowingly been carrying any fear or heaviness recently. Ask Him to do an exchange with you: what does He want to give you in place of this fear or anxiety? Ask Him if there is something that He wants you to do to intentionally choose to partner with His peace each day.

We need to lean on each other for support and encouragement in difficult seasons. If you are feeling anxious or worried, is there someone you can go to to talk about these things? Can you think of someone who is going through a difficult time to whom you could send a word of encouragement?

Set Me On Fire

'You, Lord, keep my lamp burning; my God turns my darkness into light.'

Psalm 18:28

I often hear people talking about wanting to be "on fire" for God. I have the same desire! I want to burn for Him and be full of Holy Spirit fire and boldness.

Jesus wants us to be moving in fire too. He says: *'I have come to bring fire on the earth, and how I wish it were already kindled!' (Luke 12:49)*

If we look at the disciples in Acts 2, the Holy Spirit came like tongues of fire and ignited them with fresh boldness and brightness to go out and share the good news.

When the Holy Spirit came to earth at Pentecost, He came to stay. The same Spirit is here right now with you!

But do you ever feel as though you have lost the fire? Maybe there are seasons in your life where you have been on fire for

God, but then over time, the flame grows dim. When we look at the church as a whole compared to the early church, is it actually on fire at all? Should we be doing something differently in order to keep this fire burning?

In the Old Testament tabernacle, it was the duty of the priests to keep the fire burning day and night. Now, we have the High Priest Jesus who has lit the flame and continually keeps it burning. We need to stay close to Him and we will also stay burning.

God is the one who lights the flame. He is the one who brings the fire. The fire comes from Him, not from our own strength.

It is our job to draw near to Him and to stay near to Him. Drawing near opens us up to receive His fire, and staying near allows the fire to keep burning.

If you take an ember out of the fire, it will stay burning for a little while but then will go out. This is the same with us: if we keep coming away from God's presence, we will grow dim. But if we position ourselves and live from a place of being in His presence, we will keep burning! Being "on fire" for God might look different in different seasons, but as long as we remain close to Him, we can be confident of His fiery Spirit with us.

RESPONSE

Picture Father God, Jesus and the Holy Spirit as a blazing fire. Imagine yourself drawing near to this fire and entering into it. Use your imagination. What does it feel like? What happens to you over time as you remain in this fire?

Where are you in relation to this fire right now? Have a chat to God about it. Ask Him to help you draw near to Him and remain in His fire.

Ask God to show you what being "on fire" for God looks like for you in this season. Be open to what He wants to show you about your daily walk with Him.

Jesus Is God

'Do not think that I have come to abolish the Law or the Prophets; I have come not to abolish them but to fulfil them.'

Matthew 5:17

In this verse, Jesus states that He came to fulfil the Law and the Prophets. He dies as the perfect sacrifice for sin so that in His resurrection, we can be free and share in His inheritance and eternal life.

The Bible Project's brilliant mission statement is: '*We help people experience the Bible as a unified story that leads to Jesus*'. [3]

The Bible really is a unified story where every part is pointing to Jesus! Here are some examples of where descriptions of Jesus in the New Testament match the descriptions of God in the Old Testament.

[3] The Bible Project (2024) <www.bibleproject.com>

In Job, God is described as treading on the waves of the sea:

> *'He alone stretches out the heavens and treads on the waves of the sea.' (Job 9:8)*

Then in the New Testament, we see Jesus walking on the water!

In Revelation, Jesus is described as having hair as white as wool. Read this description of God found in the Old Testament:

> *'Thrones were set in place, and the Ancient of Days took his seat. His clothing was as white as snow; the hair of his head was white like wool.' (Daniel 7:9)*

Here's another one - Jesus is described as having a voice like the sound of rushing waters in Revelation. In Ezekiel, this is what the God of Israel sounds like:

> *'I saw the glory of the God of Israel coming from the east. His voice was like the roar of rushing waters, and the land was radiant with his glory.' (Ezekiel 43:2)*

Jesus who walked with us on the earth is God Himself, and He is the fulfilment of everything that is written in the Old Testament. How amazing!

RESPONSE

The Bible shows Jesus as fully man and fully God, so it's good to remind ourselves of both!

Take some time today to read the description of Jesus in Revelation 1:12-16. Be captivated by His splendour and holiness!

You might also want to read the story of Jesus' birth (Luke 2) and marvel at how He was born as a human just like all of us, except in a slightly more unusual setting!

Holding The Hands Of Giants

'We will not hide them from their descendants; we will tell the next generation the praiseworthy deeds of the Lord, his power, and the wonders he has done.'

Psalm 78:4

When a child holds the hand of an adult, they have to stretch up to reach someone who is taller than them. But I want to flip our perspective! What if the adult who is holding the hand of the child is actually holding the hand of a giant who is not yet fully grown?

Children are physically smaller than adults, but what would happen if we chose to see them as the people that they are growing into? What if, as we guide them and lead them in their early years, we are actually holding the hands of spiritual giants?

Whether we are in children's ministry or not, and whether we are parents or not, we all have a responsibility to raise up the next generation. Do not underestimate the importance of giving children and young people a strong spiritual foundation. It will stay with them for the rest of their lives!

> *'Start children off on the way they should go, and even when they are old they will not turn from it.' (Proverbs 22:6)*

The kingdom of God is intergenerational. We need mothers and fathers who are raising up the next generation of giants. We mustn't be precious about our roles or our leadership, but we must use our positions to advocate for and call out the gold in the next generation.

If we give opportunities to our children and young people and make space for them to use their gifts, they may sometimes get things wrong. At first, they may not do things as well as we may do them. They may do things totally differently to the way we'd do them! Are we okay with that?

This is how a move of God can be sustainable. Revival was never meant to be carried by one generation. It's a family affair!

Spiritual giants are rising up all around us in our children and young people. Can you spot them?

RESPONSE

Think about the children and young people around you. Perhaps they are your children, your nieces and nephews, or children at your church. Ask God if there is something you can do today to encourage them in their walk with God.

How can you take a lead in prioritising children and young people in your church and encouraging them in their gifts? Is there a way in which you are serving or contributing in your church that you could invite the children into? What are their gifts and talents and how can you create opportunities to allow them to develop these things in your church or community?

Ask God to expand your vision to see beyond your own lifetime and to dream about something that will outlive you. If you can accomplish everything that you want to do by yourself or in your lifetime, is your dream too small?

Clothed In Christ

'So in Christ Jesus you are all children of God through faith, for all of you who were baptised into Christ have clothed yourselves with Christ.'

Galatians 3:26-27

In Matthew 22, Jesus tells a parable of a wedding banquet where all the original invitees rejected the king's invitation.

Instead, the king sent the servants out and they *'gathered all the people they could find, the bad as well as the good, and the wedding hall was filled with guests.' (Matthew 22:10)*

Unfortunately, one person didn't wear the wedding garments, so he was thrown out!

At wedding banquets in the time of Jesus, the clothes that the guests had to wear were provided by the hosts and the guests were required to wear them in order to participate in the celebration. They were usually simple robes meaning all the guests were on an equal level.

Maybe the man that refused to wear the wedding garment was wearing scruffy clothes and felt he wasn't worthy of the king's robes. Or maybe he was the richest person there and was wearing expensive clothes to flaunt his wealth! Maybe he just didn't like the colour of the robes and had a different opinion to the king. Whatever the case, any clothing apart from the king's choice was not fit for the wedding.

This is a great picture of the kingdom of heaven because it shows that we have to enter the kingdom on God's terms, not on our own. The only way into the kingdom is through Jesus and being clothed in Him.

I like the visual image of being clothed in Christ. The verse at the top says that when we are baptised, we are fully clothed in Jesus. We are given new, clean garments of salvation and righteousness.

When we are clothed in Christ, our identity is found in Him. When we submit to His perfect ways, we are fully encased in Him and we display Him wherever we go!

RESPONSE

Take some time to read the story of the wedding banquet in Matthew 22:1-14. What does the Holy Spirit want to highlight to you? What can you learn about Jesus from this passage? What can you learn about the kingdom of heaven?

Close your eyes and imagine Jesus giving you some clothes that are specifically made for you. What garments has King Jesus given you to wear? What colour are your clothes? Are there any details and patterns on the cloth? Has He given you any accessories? What do these things mean? What qualities of Christ are you displaying as you wear these clothes?

The verse at the top talks about us being clothed in Christ when we are baptised. Have you been baptised? If not, would you like to be? Who could you talk to about this?

Who Do You Say I Am?

'"But what about you?" he asked. "Who do you say I am?"'

Matthew 16:15

In his book 'The Knowledge of the Holy', A. W. Tozer wrote: *'What comes into our minds when we think about God is the most important thing about us.'* [4]

C.S. Lewis wrote a counter argument saying: *'How God thinks of us is not only more important, but infinitely more important'*! [5]

I think both what we think of God and what He thinks of us are important and connected. What God says about us and

---

[4] A. W. Tozer (1965) *'The Knowledge of the Holy: The Attributes of God, Their Meaning in the Christian Life'*

[5] C. S. Lewis (1941) *'The Weight of Glory'*

our knowledge of our identity affects how we live and relate to others. Also, what we believe about who God is will affect our choices and attitude every day.

In many ways, it doesn't really matter who we are or what we can do. God can work wonders through anybody with a willing spirit. In the Bible, God continually worked through people who put their faith in Him. It does matter who we say God is.

Many Christians don't need convincing that God is real, but our faith is still tested every day in relation to what we believe about God. Small lies can creep in from our experiences, and if we're not careful, these can grow over time and skew our perception of God away from biblical truth.

It's important that we base what we believe and say about God on the Bible. I can read that Jesus is the Prince of Peace *(Isaiah 9:6)*. First, I choose to believe it! This is where I set the bar. Then I can then let my experience of God unfold in line with this and see that each day, He truly is my source of peace.

I can read in the Bible that Jesus is the fairest among ten thousand *(Song of Songs 5:10)*. I believe it! Then day by day I can grow to experience this truth as well, that there really is no one better.

Don't wait until God proves Himself to believe it. Set your faith on the truth in the Bible, and then be delighted as He reveals His character in alignment with what He says.

RESPONSE

Think about some of the names and descriptions of God in the Bible. Here are some examples: Source of Wisdom *(Proverbs 2:6)*, Healer *(Psalm 103:3)*, Provider *(Philippians 4:19)*, Helper / Advocate / Comforter *(John 14:16)*, Strong Tower *(Proverbs 18:10)*, Compassionate and Gracious God *(Psalm 86:15)*. What others can you think of?

Meditate on these names of God. Ask God to show you a picture of Himself as each of these things. Where have you seen God reveal Himself as these different things in your life? Is there a particular facet of God's character that you would like to experience more or on a deeper level? Ask Him about that.

You Are A Resource

'Command them to do good, to be rich in good deeds, and to be generous and willing to share. In this way they will lay up treasure for themselves as a firm foundation for the coming age, so that they may take hold of the life that is truly life'

1 Timothy 6:18-19

The verse above talks about laying a firm foundation through generosity, giving and good deeds. The world would say that building a firm foundation for the future is about investing and saving. But the foundation talked about in this verse is an eternal one that continues well beyond our life on this earth. It only really makes sense if we have an eternal perspective!

I used to struggle when it came to my attitude to money. I had a mindset of lack so I would always overthink my spending, often feel guilty about spending anything on myself, and generosity towards others seemed like a stretch.

God quite radically set me free from this poverty mindset as well as it being a journey I have had to walk out through intentionality.

When I got to the root of my seeing money as an idol, generosity became a joy and something much more natural because it flowed from my relationship with God and my identity in Him, rather than from being in slavery to money.

Jesus says it clearly: *'You cannot serve both God and money.' (Luke 16:13)*

I also no longer felt guilty for spending and using my money because I saw it as a resource to be used rather than something just to store up.

You can pour more water into a river rather than a pool. If we are like a river - pouring out, stewarding well and having the mindset of being a resource — that's something God can pour into.

When we have an eternal, kingdom mindset, we have a different idea of what it means to be rich. The world may say that being rich is having a lot of money, but for us in the kingdom, whether we have money or not, we can be rich in our relationships with others and rich towards God.

David said: *'Everything comes from you, and we have given you only what comes from your hand.' (1 Chronicles 29:14)*

After all, everything we have belongs to God anyway!

RESPONSE

What does your relationship with money look like? In your life, would you say that money is a focus, a goal, a driving force, a source of worry or something that is always on your mind? If you find that perhaps you have been "serving" money in any of these ways, ask God to show you the root of this problem. Perhaps you have been believing a lie through a circumstance or person that has affected your relationship with money. Ask God what He has to say about this. What truth does God want to show you instead?

Do you see yourself as a resource? Ask God to show you how you are a resource. What is it that you have (money, areas of gifting, time, spaces etc.) that can be resources to benefit others and increase the growth of the kingdom of God? How does God want you to use these things?

Abiding

'I am the vine; you are the branches. If you remain in me and I in you, you will bear much fruit; apart from me you can do nothing.'

John 15:5

John 15 is a well known passage where Jesus talks about remaining in the vine, about pruning and about bearing fruit.

There are only really two things that He asks us to do in this passage: remain in Him and obey His commands by loving each other.

God is the one who does the pruning. He is the one who causes the fruit to grow. All we need to do is abide, be obedient, and love.

When we abide, we let ourselves be surrounded and engulfed by God. We can come just as we are, and He does the work.

In a season of pruning, we shouldn't be alarmed if we feel we are confronted with our shortcomings. Certain things that have grown a bit out of shape might be coming to our attention because they are becoming unattached! We notice them, and then in the presence of God they can fall away, leaving us with the capacity to bear more fruit.

It's also important to recognise that we can't produce fruit by trying really hard! The fruits of the Spirit naturally grow when we are in submission to the Holy Spirit. When we spend time abiding, we are transformed to look more like Jesus. When the branches are connected to the vine, what flows through Him will also flow through us.

So, we can't prune ourselves; we must stay submitted to the gardener. And we can't produce fruit by ourselves; we must stay completely plugged in to the vine.

So abide in Jesus, keep His commands, and love each other! He'll take care of the rest.

RESPONSE

Take some time to read John 15:1-17. Read it slowly and ask the Holy Spirit to highlight one part to you. Take some time to digest and reflect on what God is showing you. How does this affect your choices and how you live? How does this affect your day today?

Do you ever find yourself trying to prune yourself? Are you overly critical of yourself? Ask Jesus to show you how He sees you at this moment in your discipleship and growth. Meditate on this verse:

> *'He who began a good work in you will carry it on to completion until the day of Christ Jesus.' (Philippians 1:6)*

Do you ever find yourself trying hard to produce fruit? Take some time to close your eyes and imagine yourself as a branch that is connected to Jesus. See how the branch naturally produces fruit when it is connected to the good vine. Experience the peace that comes from knowing that you are rooted in Jesus.

The Greatest

'For those who exalt themselves will be humbled, and those who humble themselves will be exalted.'

Matthew 23:12

In Mark 9, there is a rich series of stories going from the transfiguration to the disciples being unable to cast out a demon, to them arguing about who is the greatest.

It says in Mark 9:33-34, '*When he [Jesus] was in the house, he asked them, "What were you arguing about on the road?" But they kept quiet because on the way they had argued about who was the greatest.*'

Jesus knew full well what they were arguing about! With a simple question (and probably a subtle smile), He drops it into the conversation. I can imagine the disciples looking around at each other wondering what to say or hoping someone else would answer!

To be honest, given the previous events, I can kind of see why they were arguing. Peter, James and John had just been chosen to accompany Jesus up the mountain where they had a life changing experience in seeing the transfiguration, while the other disciples were left behind and seemingly "failed" when it came to casting out a demon.

I can imagine Peter, James and John were feeling pretty smug and were maybe thinking, "Well, if I had been there I would have been able to cast out the demon!" The other disciples were probably wrestling with some self doubt, wondering why they had not been chosen to go up the mountain and wondering what had happened up there.

Jesus doesn't chastise them for arguing, but He brings it up in order to teach them a lesson.

> *'Anyone who wants to be first must be the very last, and the servant of all.' (Mark 9:35)*

This teaching is so upside down and back to front in comparison to what we are taught in the world. We are so swayed by power, success and human affirmation, but it is good to be reminded of Jesus' words. It is not about becoming great, but about becoming more like Him.

RESPONSE

Have a read of Mark 9. Can you identify with the feelings of any of the disciples? Have you ever found yourself feeling "greater" than others because of something you have done or been part of? Or have you ever felt lesser than someone else because of something you have not been able to do or something you missed out on? Take some time to think about how you felt in any of these situations. What does Jesus have to say about this?

Remind yourself of what Jesus has said about you or how He sees you. Maybe there are words that have been spoken over you in the past about your identity, or verses from the Bible that you hold on to about how God sees you. Remind yourself that these things never change no matter what you do or don't do.

In Your Midst

'Once, on being asked by the Pharisees when the kingdom of God would come, Jesus replied, "The coming of the kingdom of God is not something that can be observed, nor will people say, 'Here it is,' or 'There it is,' because the kingdom of God is in your midst."'

Luke 17:20-21

God's kingdom isn't some distant place in the sky that one day will dramatically invade earth. It already is invading earth from the inside out. It is a kingdom that is already established where Jesus is the victorious King, and it is constantly infiltrating every area of the earth.

Jesus told a parable about the kingdom of God being like yeast:

'The kingdom of heaven is like yeast that a woman took and mixed into about sixty

> *pounds of flour until it worked all through the dough.' (Matthew 13:33)*

You don't mix flour and water and then sprinkle the yeast on at the end to make bread. The yeast has to work from the inside out in order to make it rise.

This is what Jesus did: *'The Word became flesh and made his dwelling among us.' (John 1:14)*

He set up camp in the midst of us. Jesus influenced the world from the inside out.

That's also what we are called to do. We have the Holy Spirit in us and every time we recognise this, see things from God's perspective, position ourselves in alignment with what He is doing and act according to heaven's realities, we are increasing His kingdom.

If you're making bread with yeast, when you start mixing it all together and kneading it, you can't see the yeast any more. You can't specifically pick out a bit of yeast, but you can see the effects of the yeast over time when the air bubbles start to form.

I find this is often the case in my life. It is when I take a step back and look at circumstances in retrospect that I can see how God has been moving. Sometimes it is not always immediately obvious, but then I remember what I have prayed and I think about that "coincidence" and I realise that the kingdom of God really is in my midst!

RESPONSE

Jesus calls us to be set apart as representatives of His kingdom while we are in this world. (Read John 17:14-16) What are the places and spaces that you are positioned in where you are representing the kingdom of God to the world? How are your life and words a witness to the people around you? Think about people and places you are involved with outside of churches or Christian circles.

Think back over your week. Where have you seen the kingdom of God in your midst? Where have you seen God moving? Where have you seen answered prayers? Take a moment to thank God for these things!

Remember

'Tell it to your children, and let your children tell it to their children, and their children to the next generation.'

Joel 1:3

There were a lot of altars in the Old Testament. I like looking at their names and purposes.

In Judges 6:24, after he had been visited by the angel of the Lord, *'Gideon built an altar to the Lord there and called it The Lord Is Peace.'*

In Exodus 17:15, *'Moses built an altar and called it The Lord is my Banner'*, after the victory against the Amalekites where Moses held his staff up throughout the battle.

In Joshua 22:34, the Reubenites, Gadites, and the half tribe of Manasseh built an altar and called it, *'A Witness Between Us—that the Lord is God.'* It was a sign to Israel that even though those tribes had moved across the Jordan, they still served the same God.

I can think back to metaphorical "altars" or marker points of God's goodness in my life. For example, I can remember a specific time when the Lord showed me He was my Liberator. It's a marker in my life that I can remember and lean on. I can think of another time when He showed Himself to be my Provider. Looking back on this brings me peace and hope for the future.

Something that struck me about these altars in the Old Testament was that they were built for future generations. They were built to last. They were like signposts so that the descendants that followed would be able to see what the Lord had done in years gone by.

In the case of Moses' altar, the Lord told him to make sure Joshua heard about what happened when he was leading the battle *(Exodus 17:14)*. It was important for Joshua to know and remember this victory of God when eventually he led the next generation of Israelites into the promised land.

In the case of the altar in Joshua 22, the altar wasn't for themselves, but it was specifically made to last for future generations so that all the tribes of Israel would know they served the same God and had their share in Israel.

We need to remember the things that God has done for us so that we can tell them to future generations. Our ceiling must become the floor that the next generation stands upon.

Let's give future generations a solid foundation by making sure we share and proclaim the fulfilled promises and miracles of God that we can testify to!

RESPONSE

Think about the "altars" and marker points in your life: times when you have seen God's goodness, salvation, provision etc. If you haven't already, maybe you could write these down! They are precious markers from your walk with God, and you never know when you might need to lean on them in the future.

As you think about your "altars" and markers in your life, do you have testimonies of God's goodness that you could share with others to encourage them? Ask God if there is a particular way in which you can share the testimonies of your life. Does He want you to write something, record a video to share, or share a good news story over coffee with a friend?

Slipstreaming God

'The Lord himself goes before you and will be with you; he will never leave you nor forsake you. Do not be afraid; do not be discouraged.'

Deuteronomy 31:8

Recently, I was in York with my family. It was a sunny afternoon so it was busy pretty much anywhere we went, but to get to where we were going, we decided to walk down the Shambles. Now, if you don't know, the Shambles is a historic street that is notoriously busy and crowded with tourists. It's an incredibly narrow street too which makes it even more difficult to pass through!

I don't really like crowds, so as we began to make our way down the street, I tucked in behind my Dad. He paved the way and parted a route through the people! As long as I stuck behind him and followed his steps, the route was easy for me.

However, halfway down the street, I allowed a bit of distance to come between me and my Dad. This space was soon flooded with people and I was separated from him, meaning I had to try and forge my own path through the bustling tourists!

When I emerged from the crowd on the other side, after taking a brief moment to recover, I thought about how this is a great picture of walking with God.

God loves to help us. He is very happy to take the lead! He is very happy for us to tuck in behind Him and let Him make the way. If we stay close to Him and follow in His footsteps, our route will be much more simple!

But if we allow distance to come between us and Him, we can still try to move forward, but it will be much more difficult. Trying to make a way by ourselves is much more tiring and strenuous. It is much better to let our more than capable God open up the way!

So let's walk in the shadow of our Father God. Let's follow closely in the footsteps of Jesus. Let's be guided by the Holy Spirit in the path we should take.

RESPONSE

First of all, take some time to rest in the shadow of God. Take refuge in His presence and take comfort in His nearness.

Use your imagination to picture yourself following Jesus and walking in His footsteps. Let the scenario unfold. Where is He taking you? How can you keep close to Him as you pass through different terrain? What is He saying to you as you follow Him?

What path is the Holy Spirit carving out for you in this season? How can you follow His lead today and in the days to come? Is He nudging you or prompting you in a particular direction? Is He encouraging you to keep pressing on in the direction you are going?

Great Expectations

'God's voice thunders in marvellous ways; he does great things beyond our understanding.'

Job 37:5

I love to dream big! I love to use my imagination to think about the future and the things that God might have in store. However, because I have a bit of an overactive imagination, it sometimes means that things don't turn out quite as I envisioned!

Maybe that means I should just have low expectations. That way, I can't be disappointed. I can only be pleased if something exceeds my expectations, or just remain content if it doesn't. Maybe it is safer to not dream too big so I don't expose myself to the risk of disappointment.

I don't think that is the best way to approach things. I believe God loves it when we dream and pray big prayers, and it is important to live and move from a place of hope.

However, I believe we must be careful when it comes to expectations. The verse above says that God does things beyond our understanding. Expectations, whether big or small, essentially put God in a box. We should still dream and use our imagination, but we should allow ourselves to be open to *how* God wants to do something.

When Joseph had his dreams of greatness, I bet he didn't expect that God would use the route of slavery and prison to take him there!

When the Israelites in the wilderness thought of entering the promised land, I bet they didn't expect they would be marching round the walls of Jericho and seeing them fall before their eyes!

We must hold fast to God's promises. But we must not hold fast to our expectations of *how* He will fulfil them.

We must let go of our expectations of God and instead, just be *expectant* to see Him move.

If we have too many plans or preconceived ideas about exactly how we think something will happen, we may not be open and flexible enough to go with His ways, or we may miss Him moving all together.

We must instead live in relationship with God so we can go with His plans and ways of doing things. We can't try too hard to get ready, but we must live ready.

RESPONSE

Think about something you are praying for at the moment, or think of a promise from God that you are holding onto. Ask God if you have perhaps unknowingly placed any expectations on this prayer or promise about exactly how it will happen. You might want to write down this prayer or promise and place it in front of you to symbolise placing it into God's hands. As you do, release the control to Him. Hold on to hope for the actual prayer or promise, but ask God to help you to lay down any preconceived expectations about how He will do something.

Have you experienced disappointment in your life? Ask God if He wants to highlight a specific time when you have been disappointed. Come before Jesus and ask Him where He was in this time. Ask Him if this disappointment has affected how you now see Him or how you see your life. Is there a truth that He wants to give you instead?

Again? Seriously?

'Master, we've worked hard all night and haven't caught anything. But because you say so, I will let down the nets.'

Luke 5:5

Peter had been fishing all night and had not caught anything. He had worked hard and had thrown his nets out time and time again, fighting the thoughts of giving up after many failed attempts. However, it got to a point where because of the lack of fish and the long hours he had worked, Peter knew it wasn't really worth trying again. He headed back to the shore to wash his nets so he could head home to get some needed rest. What else could he do?

Then Jesus tells him to let the nets down and catch some fish.

That must have been completely laughable and even offensive to the exhausted Peter.

"Again? Seriously? Do you even know what I've been doing all night?"

There may be times in our lives when we feel daunted by the thought of going again, whatever that thing might be for you. We might feel so worn out that even considering trying one more time seems exhausting. Maybe it's just too overwhelming to think about praying again, believing again, or hoping again.

Peter had probably seen Jesus around before this particular encounter and might have heard Him teach and perform miracles. However, in this moment of exhaustion and frustration, I can imagine that the thought of taking the boat out again was the exact opposite of what he wanted to do.

But Peter looked at the face of Jesus. He could see there was hope in His eyes and kindness in His smile. Yes, something was different about this man. So he did go again... and it changed his life.

If you feel that Jesus is asking you to go again, don't look out to the lake as you might get overwhelmed. Don't look at your empty nets as you may get discouraged. First look at Jesus, and He'll give you what you need to go again.

RESPONSE

Is there an area in which you feel Jesus is asking you to persevere or try again? How do you feel about that right now? Talk about these feelings with Jesus.

Is there something that you are focussing on that is making you reluctant to persevere or try again? Maybe it is past disappointment, your current circumstances, not knowing where to start, or just feeling exhausted. Bring this thing before Jesus, but then choose to look at His face. What does He want to say? What does He want to give you to help you?

Peter had to take the very first step of getting back into the boat before he saw the miraculous catch of fish. What is the very first step that Jesus wants you to take?

I Need You

'Humble yourselves, therefore, under God's mighty hand.'
1 Peter 5:6

In difficult and testing times, this is when we often know our need for God and we may naturally turn to Him for help and strength. But when we are catching the waves and cruising along nicely, this is when we so often must remind ourselves that we need Jesus.

In the Beatitudes, Jesus says: *'Blessed are the poor in spirit, for theirs is the kingdom of heaven.' (Matthew 5:3)*

Another way to phrase this verse is to say: "Blessed are those who recognise their need for God, for theirs is the kingdom of heaven."

It's in the good times that we can so easily forget that we *need* God! We may feel strong enough to rely on our own strength and character, but soon this will cause us to become independent and distanced from Him.

There are some sobering verses in Malachi of how the people of Israel forgot their need for God and took His grace for granted. They abused their relationship with Him because they got too confident in themselves.

> *'You have wearied the Lord with your words.*
> *"How have we wearied him?" you ask. By saying,*
> *"All who do evil are good in the eyes of the Lord,*
> *and he is pleased with them"'* (Malachi 2:17)

'Will a mere mortal rob God? Yet you rob me.' (Malachi 3:8)

Can we make God weary? Can humans rob God? Yet that is what God said the people were doing. It is because God is so involved with us that He is so concerned. A distant god wouldn't care, but our God cares because He loves us and He's so close to us.

The fact that He cares so deeply means that it's not only our sin that affects God, but it is our good choices as well. It is wonderful to think that we can delight and please our Father with our presence, choices and character.

So, let's remain thankful always. I don't want to forget my need for God or His free gift of grace.

RESPONSE

Make a list of some specific things that you are thankful for today. How has God helped you, provided for you, comforted you or defended you this week? How can you continue to remain thankful in the days and weeks to come?

Where have you needed to lean on God recently? Where have you recognised your need for Him? Delight in His strength and readiness to support you.

Take a moment to rejoice in God's pleasure over you. You delight Him! Ask Him what He loves about you!

Bold Faith

'Now faith is confidence in what we hope for and assurance about what we do not see.'

Hebrews 11:1

Some verses in the Bible can be so familiar that we forget what they actually say. They can easily become a string of sounds that we don't really process!

As I was reading the above verse the other day, I didn't think too much about it because it's quite a familiar verse. Then I had to read it again. Hang on, what is this verse *actually* saying?

To be confident in something that we don't see or haven't seen yet seems a bit of a challenge!

To have faith in the existence of God is one thing, but perhaps if you have been a Christian for a long time, or even a short time, you will have seen, heard and experienced His goodness and love.

But what about having faith for things that we haven't seen? Can we have the boldness to believe for something just because it is in alignment with God's promises, even if we've never seen it?

An example of this great faith in the Bible was from the centurion whose servant was sick. *(Matthew 8: 5-13)*

Jesus offered, *'Shall I come and heal him?'* But the centurion said, *'Just say the word, and my servant will be healed'*.

The centurion had such confidence in something that hadn't happened yet. There is no record of Jesus healing someone remotely in the gospel of Matthew up until then. However, the centurion still had faith because he had confidence in Jesus. He recognised Jesus' authority and power. Jesus was delighted by the centurion's faith and was willing to go along with his request.

It has been famously said by John Wimber that faith is spelled R-I-S-K. The centurion took a risk in asking for something that he had no solid evidence for, but his strong faith didn't go unnoticed.

RESPONSE

We can't force ourselves to have faith, but when we saturate ourselves in the Word of God, faith will rise.

Paul says: *'Faith comes from hearing the message, and the message is heard through the word about Christ.' (Romans 10:17)*

So, think about something miraculous that was recorded somewhere in the Bible. Maybe it is a story of Jesus healing someone in the gospels, or a miraculous prison escape in Acts, or a time where God saved His people in an Old Testament battle. Have a read of this story and meditate on God's power today. What can you learn about God from this story? Take heart in His strength.

Let God Do His Thing

'Now to him who is able to do immeasurably more than all we ask or imagine, according to his power that is at work within us, to him be glory'
Ephesians 3:20-21

Ultimately, there is nothing that we can do without God. He holds everything together and all life is in His hands.

'Apart from me you can do nothing.' (John 15:5)

But, He has also given us gifts and talents. He has given us ability. As God ultimately holds everything together, there are some things that we could do in our own strength. We might take stock of our gifts and abilities and experience and think, "Yes, I can tackle that challenge. I'm qualified to do this. It might stretch me a bit, but it's within the realm of my capability."

But if we only ever choose to do things that we know we can do by ourselves, are we really letting God be God in our lives? If we are completely self-sufficient, we miss out on being able to lean on God for support. We ignore the provision that He wants to be able to give us!

I think God quite likes being God. I think He enjoys being a good Father to His children. He loves it when we lean on Him for support. He loves it when we make room for Him to move in our lives!

I think there are two things to learn here. First of all, even though God has given us an ability to choose and to do things, ultimately everything is in His hands. We must retain this healthy perspective. He is God, not us!

> *'Do you have an arm like God's, and can your voice thunder like his?' (Job 40:9)*

> *'As the heavens are higher than the earth, so are my ways higher than your ways and my thoughts than your thoughts.' (Isaiah 55:9)*

Secondly, I want to call us to live a life that makes room for God to move. Our dreams must be big enough so that we can't actually do them on our own. If you can accomplish your dreams by yourself, dream bigger! Allow God to be God!

RESPONSE

Take stock of your ideas, dreams and ambitions. Take a moment to bring these before God.

Can you do these things by yourself? If the success of your dreams depends on your own capability to accomplish them, do you need to think bigger?

Think about the things that you are doing at the moment. Take a moment to lay them down before God. Ask God to highlight to you anywhere that you are leaning too much on your own strength at the moment. Ask Him to help you to lean on His strength in these things. How does He want you to do this?

He Sees, He Knows, He Feels

'The Word became flesh and made his dwelling among us.'
John 1:14

I want to invite you to take comfort in our God who is not estranged from us. He sees us, He knows us, and He feels too. I want to invite you to take some time to read this slowly, becoming aware of God with you right now. Pause when you need to. Relax into His love.

He sees.

> *'For the eyes of the Lord are on the righteous and his ears are attentive to their prayer.' (1 Peter 3:12)*

Take a moment right now where you are just to become aware of His eyes on you. Remember that they are eyes of love and delight! His disposition towards you is favourable and protective.

Take comfort in His loving gaze on you. His proud Father gaze!

He knows.

> *'You know when I sit and when I rise; you perceive my thoughts from afar. You discern my going out and my lying down; you are familiar with all my ways.' (Psalm 139:2-3)*

He handcrafted every part of you. He knows you better than you know yourself. He knows your ways and your tendencies. He knows your strengths and weaknesses. He knows your motives and your desires. And He loves you deeply.

He feels.

> *'He was despised and rejected by mankind, a man of suffering, and familiar with pain.' (Isaiah 53:3)*

One of the most incredible and unfathomable parts of our God is that He feels. The God of the universe feels deeply.

Jesus lived a rich life on earth full of laughter, joy and friendship. But He also experienced suffering, pain, temptation, rejection, loneliness and betrayal. He identifies with all of those things and everything in between. His compassion and empathy is boundless.

God is on the journey of life with us. We have an intimate God. We have a God that comes close: closer than anyone else. We have a God who sees, knows and feels.

RESPONSE

You might want to read Genesis 16 and the story of Hagar. Hagar gave God the name: *'The God who sees me' (Genesis 16:13)* In Hagar's grief and despair, God was with her. Is there anything that the Holy Spirit wants to highlight to you in this passage? What does He want you to know?

Whatever you are going through at the moment, bring this before Jesus. Maybe you need to weep with Him. Maybe you need to laugh with Him. Maybe you need to talk with Him. Maybe you need to just sit with Him. Take comfort in His nearness and His understanding.

The Power Of The Cross

'For the message of the cross is foolishness to those who are perishing, but to us who are being saved it is the power of God.'

1 Corinthians 1:18

In the verse above, we can see that the power of God is in the message of the cross. This is good news for us because it means we don't need to try and muster up power and impact with persuasive words! The message of the cross already contains power. Whenever and wherever the cross is spoken about, the power of God is at work.

Paul writes: *'When I came to you, I did not come with eloquence or human wisdom as I proclaimed to you the testimony about God. For I resolved to know nothing while I was with you except Jesus Christ and him crucified.' (1 Corinthians 2:1-2)*

Paul didn't need to try hard to make the gospel exciting. It already is! Paul's evangelism strategy was just to live, breathe and speak of Jesus and let the Holy Spirit do the rest.

Jesus Christ, the son of God, came to earth and was crucified by those He created. The good news is that He was raised to life again after three days, victorious over all sin and death! Our salvation, healing and freedom are all paid for, and now we get to step into the glorious fullness of life that Jesus offers. There is the power!

Some people can be hostile to the gospel depending on where they are at in their journey, but this doesn't mean in any way that we should try to water down, soften or mould the gospel to their expectations or wants in order to make it more palatable.

Yes, we should always have wisdom when telling people about Jesus, and evangelism is never about force feeding truth or getting argumentative. What we need to remember is that we can trust the message of the cross. It is not our job to come up with a persuasive story, but we can trust that there is already power in God's story.

This is an encouragement to us, because it doesn't matter who we are or what we are good at, but we can all share this message. We just need to trust that God is at work. He is the one who works in the hearts of His children and He draws people to Himself.

RESPONSE

Take some time today to re-read or reflect on the message of the cross. Why not take communion today as a reminder of Jesus' sacrifice for you? Allow yourself to be moved by the power of the gospel.

Is there a particular way in which God wants you to share the message of the cross today or this week? See if He is highlighting a particular way in which you could do this. You might want to pray and ask God to give you opportunities this week where you can share the good news of Jesus with those around you.

We're All Involved

'Consecrate yourselves, for tomorrow the Lord will do amazing things among you.'

Joshua 3:5

The book of Joshua is an exciting story of a whole nation entering into the promises that God had for them. After Moses died, Joshua led the people, first crossing the river Jordan miraculously on dry land, then defeating the entire city of Jericho in the strength and power of God.

Multiple times in the book of Joshua, the words 'whole nation' are used.

For example: *'All Israel passed by until the whole nation had completed the crossing on dry ground.' (Joshua 3:17)*

I wonder how long that would have taken!

When the Israelites crossed the Jordan to enter the promised land, every single person crossed that river. Joshua didn't just take the armed men across until it was safe for everyone to come. It was the mothers holding their babies, the children, the teenagers, the elderly, and all the people in between who crossed that river on dry ground. Each one of them was caught up right in the centre of this miracle of God.

Now is a good time to get ready not just to see amazing stories reported in the next town or city or on the news, but to expect to see the Lord do amazing things amongst us: things that will affect our families, friendship groups, churches and communities, and things that will involve every single one of us, from the young to the old.

Right before the Israelites cross the river, Joshua says to them:

> *'Consecrate yourselves, for tomorrow the Lord will do amazing things among you.' (Joshua 3:5)*

Now is also a good time to prepare ourselves for what God is going to do amongst us. It is a time to awaken and be engaged with the things of heaven and the agenda of God. It's a time to clear our senses so that we might be sensitive to the move of the Holy Spirit. It's a time to pray and to commit ourselves afresh to God.

Be encouraged because Jesus, the Light of the World, is in you! And get ready, because God is moving among you!

RESPONSE

Ask God how He wants you to get ready at this time. What does it look like for you to consecrate yourself? Has God been highlighting anything to you recently that you need to do or deal with?

Read these words from Isaiah: *'Arise, shine, for your light has come, and the glory of the Lord rises upon you. See, darkness covers the earth and thick darkness is over the peoples, but the Lord rises upon you and his glory appears over you.' (Isaiah 60:1-2)*

Ask God today, what does it look like for you to arise and shine in your area, your workplace, your community or with your church? Where does He want you to start to move? What part do you play in an intergenerational move of God?

I sincerely hope you enjoyed reading this book and going deeper in your relationship with God.

If you liked this one, you will probably enjoy my first book, '40 Days of Delighting in God'. It contains 40 more devotions to delve into!

40 Days of Delighting in God:
ISBN (paperback): 978-1-7395233-0-5
ISBN (eBook): 978-1-7395233-1-2

Contact the author: mary@maryswain.co.uk
More about Mary: www.maryswain.co.uk